LIVING

WITH

WOLVES

LIVING
WITH
WOLVES

Poems

Anne Haven McDonnell

Split Rock Press
Washburn, Wisconsin
2020

ISBN 978-1-7354839-0-0

Cover and layout design: Crystal S. Gibbins

Split Rock Press is dedicated to publishing eco-friendly books that explore place, environment, and the relationship between humans and the natural world. Visit us online at www.splitrockreview.org/press.

Environmental consciousness is important to us. This book is printed with chlorine-free ink and acid-free paper stock supplied by a Forest Stewardship Council certified provider. The paper stock is made from 30% post-consumer waste recycled material.

ACKNOWLEDGMENTS

My gratitude to the wolves, the island, and to my friends, family, and strangers who shared their stories.

Thanks to the editors of the publications in which versions of these poems first appeared.

About Place Journal, Political Landscapes Issue: "The Farmer" (as "A Sea Inside")

Dark Mountain: "The Flute Player" (as "Predators")

The Learned Pig: "Creation Story"

Terrain.org: "At Swamp's Edge" (as "Swamp's Edge"), "A Thin Line," "The Lost Girl," "The Swimmers," "The Study," and "How to Sit with a Wolf"

These poems are inspired from experiences and interviews collected in a community who lives with wolves on an island in British Columbia.

TABLE OF CONTENTS

Prologue: A Creation Story

There was a loneliness
spread so thin
that no one named it.
She collected her dead around her, missing
the dead she never knew.
The ravens remembered all
the dead, and they catapulted
down shafts of wind, ragged plummets
before swerving up and laughing on thermals.
They tried to tell her, chortling
their watery croaks from telephone poles.
She only answered with more questions.
Or she kept driving to another parking lot,
late again. In another place, the raven people
still traveled with wolves, diving
to play with pups and calling
out seal carcasses.
Where the ravens went, the wolves followed.
Where the wolves ran, the ravens flew.
Long ago, this was agreed upon, and nothing
could break it. Even now,
in the lands that have forgotten,
with the people who have forgotten,
in the cities that have forgotten,
the ravens perch in the branches
of the old trees who have seen it all.
The ravens wait for the wolves.
Finally, she traveled to an island in the north,
and she learned from a raven who came
each morning for scraps left on a flat rock.
Across the shoreline where the raven soared
and stitched the air, she looked up
as the wolves looked up,
and something old was born.

The Swimmers

After all the wolves on the island were killed by cyanide, traps, and bullets, decades later, wolves from the mainland swam for miles to repopulate the island.

By dream, by twitch, by lope, by gazing from the shore, by howls that gather,
by circle and whine, by hint, rumor and surge, by yearn, nip, and bark,
by stretch, itch, and shake, by splash, dunk, and swim by starlight,
by bull kelp and driftwood, by calm and gelatinous sea, by stink
of whale, by salt of far, by winter fur, by paws as paddles,
by chuff and nostril huff, by steam of breath above
the sea, by belly of salmon, by hunger for deer,
by memory in blood, by roam for love,
by milk and teat, by marrow and fat,
by muscle, skull and golden eyes,
by magnetic pull, by currents
and tides, by miles, by sinking
cold, with no one watching
by sea by sea by sea.

The Stories

are carried by almost everyone.
Whispered over gas pumps, traded
as currency in aisles at market.
A shadow slipping back to trees.
A white wolf at the corner of Red Rock Road.
Two black wolves, sleeping with snouts tucked
under tails in deep moss on the bluffs.
A wolf eating apples in the orchard,
slurping up seaweed, digging for clams.
The terrier that followed the howls, never
returned. The sheep torn open.

Each story has a pit to carry and turn
over: stone of worry, stone of prayer, warm
against the body, in a pocket
like the one on your thigh
as you bend to gather piles of salt-crusted
seaweed the storm left in a lumpy rope
at tide line. You fill two orange buckets, one in each
hand you carry up the trail below the bluff
to the shrinking compost. The stone
in your pocket starts its soft bleating,
almost bleeding, your skin
lit and honed, prickling
in the undergrowth. Salal berries
glowing red as meat. You step over
fresh scat—still-wet deer fur,
chips of black hoof, shards
of white bone glisten with grease.
In the forest, just beyond sight, a snap
and crack of branches charges
the air between trees. Something
sudden waits for an opening.
Above you, nighthawks thread the evening
sky with boom and whistle.
A loon in salt water wails to a loon
somewhere on the inland lake.

You finger the stone, its wave-worn
surface, its weight—the story
you carry has made you
another animal.

The Sculptor

If I was the first person on earth,
the track is like a letter. Our first drawings
in the caves were our hands—our tracks.
This island is the only place
I could have come to this.
I thought if I cast all these prints, I can know them.
Look, this one has a broken toe.
We've seen them here eating pumpkins.
They eat whatever they can get—
baby seals, clams, oysters, mink, otters, squirrels, squash.
Down on the beach, I carved two faces
out of old cedar logs. One morning
I watched them swim across. Five of them.
The little guy was the last to swim.
They waited and they put him in the middle.
Old Henry up on Bluebird Lake,
he is careful when he butchers.
After they get the taste for sheep,
they come back.

Dear Oysterman,

I am tired of your stories.
Every story needs an ear. Mine
are the only ones here in your tilted shack,
where the bluff melts back with each rising
tide. The oysters are dark and meaty
and taste like privacy.
Yes, the intertidal breathes the world.
Yes, to feed by filter, to pearl from sea.
You tell me another creation story, your beard
dripping with salt and grease.
I have paddled for miles in rain, eyed
by eagles hunched and ragged in soggy cedar.
I am hungry and cold.
Thank you for the strong coffee, black.
Thank you for the smoked oysters on toast.
You shuck and midden the shore with shells,
chalky white with a nub of flesh.
The spat take hold, overlap
in dense beds that you harvest.
Tell me the story I came for:
knee-deep in seawater, this is where
the wolves surrounded, bared their teeth
and blocked your way home.
It wasn't you, but your golden
retriever they were after.
Your voice slips below the morning glass
light, not a whisper, but smooth
with truth—that surge of fear
you wouldn't trade for anything.

The Songs

The house is a shell,
quiet and permeable.

What is the mother-tongue of forest
on the edge of low-tide sea?

We cup our ears, walls
thin as skin. We sweep

sawdust into corners, sit
on plywood in the rising

dark. Our necks bare as peeled
fruit, the house breathing in its bones.

Who can say how many? Deep
in their throats, the songs split

into strands, strange harmonics
that climb from roots

my spine knows as sorrow.
Loss and remembering, the same

churn. Howls spin into whirl,
gathering whir of shore birds,

silver flash of fish, fat
dark from the wells of trees.

The air after, sheared.
Knife-quiet.

Hold my hand, you whisper. I hold.

The Tracker Speaks

All the new-comers, do-gooders, tree-huggers
(like you) don't know shit. Nine wolves in her yard.
Come home to roost. Then they call me.
Then they buy a gun. All my life
I've followed tracks in snow. I call it
The White Pages. I don't need to read it
in books. Tracks tell me everything. I don't shoot
lightly. But wolves have lost their fear.
Not my trapline. Back in the depression, no one
had any money. We all needed deer meat.
Some set out scraps dipped in poison.
Now that's not right either. I don't shoot lightly.
Once I trapped a wolf in Otter Cove. The others stayed away.
They knew something bad happened there.
Once I followed a cougar's tracks just to see what she did.
A hollowed-out cedar log with a crack on top.
She lay inside to watch what came up the creek.
That's how cagey. I don't need others to tell me.
Wolves swam back after the beaver returned.
They like the fat.

The Flute Player

A scream is made to cut
through the mind's fog,
all rescue circuits flipped on—
any kind of baby animal will do.
When his sleep is sliced by sounds
from the gulley, deep in the woods outside,
he moves towards the *yawl*, a flashlight
tunneling into dark, searching the cry,
and he knows before he sees the tawny warm
fur, speckled white, folded in a thicket of salal.

The fawn's mouth is open, her fresh
pink tongue hanging while the cry loops
itself out from her belly from where her eyes—
wide open and hardened to whatever she sees
outside—are already living inside
wherever this cry cuts from.
What could he do?

He thinks how the sound must pull
all the blood in her mother, hidden
and waiting. The wolf must also be waiting
to finish this, listening to this cry
light up a tunnel of hunger.

Once, he played his flute across the bay,
and the wolves began to sing
to each other across the water, stitching
this island and that. Always the arc and hang
of their howls, the pull inside him towards
this sound that peeled the air, and the silence
after, the night full and undone.

He thought of carrying
that speckled fawn home but left it—
all of it—the sound of his own footsteps
through the brush all he heard in his long
walk back to the porch light he left on
in his cabin with a door that doesn't lock.

Tracks

Last night's rain
fills the mud
rim of this
track where
the wolf
with two
crooked toes
crossed
the trail
so close
to where
we spooned
in sleep—
dark tucking in
the edges
of our loose-
limbed dreaming,
bodies curved
and pressed
together
like an ear.

The Farmer

i.

Moonlit field sloping down from a thicket of alder, deeper cedar and fir forest beyond: the body of a brindled wolf lay still, dragged there by hind legs, two bullet holes in her flank, matted blood, shellacked dark fur surrounding the hole where the bullet tunneled and exploded her heart. From the window, the farmer who shot and dragged and left her there can see her form in the field, her brindled fur paler than grass in moonlight.

ii.

Another wolf, smaller and darker, sat beside her body. The moon drew an outline of the dark wolf, ears upright, head turned towards the house, a shadow of black, a magnet of night. The dark wolf had come out cautious and low, sniffed the length of her, lingering over the dried blood, and sat. The smell of her body still her and not her, her musk fading and sinking into the ground as the other smell rose and filled her form, this other smell that pinned the dark wolf beside her, as if leaving would let the smell collapse, let it flood her body and beyond her body into night itself, its closeness and its vast reach. The dark wolf had not moved, would not move until first light spilled between branches onto the field.

iii.

The moon washed over both wolves, alive and dead, with its bonelight. The moon loved both wolves equally in its cool shine. The moon threw light over all of it: behind the woods: the road, the post office, some houses with people sleeping, and behind that: three empty swings with glinting metal chains, and behind that: more forest and the maple tree with its world of leaves and arcing branches over the pile of pale driftwood tangled with black ribbons of kelp. Below this: the seeping tide, hissing its way up barnacle-covered rocks, fingering into silver rivers on the low channels of sand.

iv.

As the farmer turned from the window, he turned also from the pooling dark, rising in his chest. The dark seeped and filled like a quiet tide. He watched the field and the wolves for a long time before turning, the dark settling inside his legs and up into his belly and rising up through. It was like missing, an ache filled and rose and he thought of his daughter and her daughter sleeping in that far city and he thought of the lamb he pulled by the hooves until she slipped into the hay and he cupped his hand across her small face, pinching the blood and the liquid sac that clung there, opening nostrils and mouth and eyes to her first air. He thought of the sheep he had found behind the barn, pale skin of her belly the color of ivory or an egg, torn open and curled back so he saw the black cavity where the insides of her had been ripped and swallowed. He stopped thinking and stayed still with the dark inside him, felt it like the night itself entering him the way night enters like water rising. And finally, he turned towards sleep, as if to break the rising. As if he would not lay down in a sea of dark.

Me, the Visitor

First light, we walk barefoot
  on duff, whisper to keep
our voices inside
  what is growing
between branches. We want
  to drink it. We lick a bead
of dew off the white
  belly of a polypore. Medicine
you say. I taste dank
  rain, mushroom, sugar,
and dirt. All summer
  we searched the trails,
slept on the north end
  where they den and howl.
You swept the beach with
  a branch to wake and look
for tracks. Never seen
  unless they want to be
everyone said. You squint
  behind glasses to think
of a word, miss
  what comes round
the trail: I say
  What's —
    that—
      dog—
        doin—

A tightrope snaps
  eye to eye:
wolf   human

A half-eaten fawn leg still spotted
  with fur, dropped
where, I swear, he was—

How to Sit with a Wolf

If you are peeling chestnuts
    on the rocks above Frank's beach.
If the basket in your lap
    balances the day's
grey light, corrals
    the sky between polished stone.

If days of rain
    and more rain
have pushed newts to their slow,
    blood-chilled crawl
on the road. If yesterday
    you carried each one
across in its open-toed
    freeze, orange belly above
your open palm.

If the sea gentles here
    between islands, your fingers
work back bits of leathery skin,
    the nuts fuzzed and naked
in a blue bowl.

If you keep your eyes down—
    the song you sing
in your off-key quiver, the words
    lift and drop and lift

until the young wolf you caught
    sleeping on sand takes
you in and takes you
    for this place
you are trying
    to belong to—

The Two People at the Swamp's Edge

For C and A

He studies bat voices, slows them down
enough to hear, to draw a voice in lines.
Candlelight on the dock silvers
the surface of the swamp. A beaver slaps
her fat tail, a heron scream cuts the dark.
A small wooden bridge leads to the beach,
a rocky cove where they farm oysters,
wolves watching from the trees.

Here, on the edge of swamp and sea—
what happens when love leaves a place?
By love, I mean his hands, when they
shine a flashlight up the hollowed burn scar in an old cedar.
A motor of hundreds of tiny bat wings
crawl in the beam. By love, I mean
her hands, as they gather reeds in the canoe,
dry them in bundles, weave baskets she sells at market.

By love, I mean their hands,
when they searched behind the gravel pit,
poked sticks to spring all the traps
left there for wolves.

Huddled by solitude, they leave
offerings: carved stones hanging from hemlock,
feathers bundled with twine. He holds a tiny
bone, asks us to guess—
a crossbill's clavicle like a shard of light
held up in his fingertips. A tiny bat
skeleton, black skin, paper thin,
stretched between its wing fingers.

After twenty years, what is left
in their wake? The windows dark,
the wooden plank nailed to the alder,
empty of birdseed. A stitched line of prints—

wolf, human, raccoon, gull—
mapped the path to swamp's edge.

A Thin Line

Once, I saw a river of bats
stream like black confetti over my head,
fan out across the valley. Imagine:
their winged hands in the dark air,
their nipples and warm bellies and tiny shouts
bouncing back the geometry
of moth wings in an ocean of night.

I have a friend who placed them side by side,
two skulls meticulously cleaned: wolf and bat—
the same slide down the nose, hollowed caves
for eyes, even those curved canine teeth.
Almost identical except one could be
crushed to crumbs between two fingers.
He set them on his table made of black stone
with fossils spiraled like shooting stars.
We crouched on the floor, eye to eye, to see.

There's not much between us
on the sinewy earth. Things repeat
themselves—and then startle
in newness, the way bones are rivers
for a while, and then become riverbeds
with curves and sockets where muscles
pooled and chewed. Memory, too,
circles back, the thick resting weight
of your hands on me,
like a bat wraps her shawl of wings
around the warm planet of her heart,
the ice-light of stars a breath away.

The Trapper Speaks, Again

The wolves took my best dog.
My neighbor used to let her chickens free-range. That brings wolves.
A wolf was right here.
I draw a line in the sand and that's it.
I was thirty years old before anyone saw a wolf again.
So much of what they say is nonsense.
What is it you're doing here again?
There are two kinds of people on this island. They change their tune.
An old wolf, skinny and sick hanging around the playground. What would you do?
You don't take dogs in the bush. It's an attractor.
Oh, they're smart alright.
I think they have a place. Up to a point.
Do-gooders say wolves never attack people. An old trapper told me. He knows plenty.
I'd be more concerned about a cougar, but I wouldn't say never.
The wolves have grown too tame.
Three wolves behind his pickup.
One followed Sara home, trailing her from the trees.
Wolves don't like dogs.
They lure them in and eat.

The Lost Girl

This is what happened: Kaya wandered down beach, past the nettle patch, past the old fish trap, halfway down to oyster spit. At five-years old, she wobbled in her wander. While her family was unloading their boat, she kept wandering. Low tide, wet sand, beneath her feet, clams sealed their lips and dove deeper. Beneath her feet, purple sand dollars brushed the shallow currents with their spines. Above her head, eagles perched on hemlock tops. She must have gotten tired. She may have sung to herself as she walked. She may have sung to the crabs that scuttled from her fingers. She was not afraid. She must have looked for a dry soft place to lie down. Between two cedar trees on a bank above the beach. Sleeping there when her mother found her. *A big dog came to sit with me*, she later would say. The wolf's back haunches touched the girl's elbow where she lay sleeping. *Just watching over her*, her mother said. That's how they found her. This is what happened.

The Old Dog

We keep him close, leashed.
Each morning, I wipe a dab
of grease in his dry blind eye.
We nuzzle him between us,
worry over tumors and stiff joints.
A metal-pinned hip, mostly deaf,
but his nose keeps growing sharper.
He circles the wolf scat,
raises his head, looks blindly
into the brush off trail.
It's more than tolerance, learning
to co-exist, the wolf scientist says.
When I let him loose, he limps
ahead, rounds the bend
out of view. What would I give,
I wonder—*not this old dog*—
my breath caught, tight until
I find him again, sniffing
the edge of trail. On his last hike
to the bluffs, he lay his body down
on a pillow of deep moss. The wolves
sometimes sleep there too.

They Are Talking

In our teeth, the taste of old
metal: bullets and barbed wire,
blood and money. Grit and rust.
Fear squeezes the aperture,
chokes the back of the throat, static
in the ears. Eye in the scope, finger on the trigger,
breath caught and held. The boy,
who could blame him?

It's hard to hear what they are saying,
said the boy who used his father's rifle,
shot one. He didn't see the opening
through the trees—the one direction
the wolves left open, wanting him to go.

The wolves were showing you the way
out, Grace tells him. Herding you away
from their den. Grace heard their death
songs. Saw them rub their faces
in the dead wolf's fur and sing.

Be careful not to flirt with words,
Grace says. If you are followed,
if the wolf keeps the same distance,
if she sits, lowers and shakes
her muzzle, if she escorts you
away, she is speaking
to you. She is showing
you the way out.

The Man at the Maple Tree

We shared the meadow outside
my yurt. We shared the trails. At night,
my headlamp caught their eyes: blue-green
for wolves, yellow-orange for deer.
At night, I heard everything—dolphins
breathing in the bay. Deer munching
grass. Wolves panting as they ran.
For some reason, they left my dog alone.
One scout always watched me until
I passed the den. I watched the brindled mother
sit on a high knoll while the pups
played tug-of-war with a kelp rope.
One year they left the pups at my gate all day.
But when they start singing—
the little ones yip yip yip yip
and the low drone like a vacuum
all the hairs stand up—

The Wolf Who Didn't Leave

The woman cursed,
threw stones, waved
her arms in the sky.
Nothing but a blink,
a yawn, a trot
back a few feet
to sit and face
her again. Once upon
a time, the woman learned
this surge of fear
and thought she could carry on.
The woman cursed
this calm refusal
to shrink or move. But
the wolf on the beach sat
in her stillness, waiting.
When finally the woman turned
to leave, the wolf slipped into the trees,
returned with three
small pups trailing
behind her to splash
and play in the sea.
Now that you have heard
this story, what will you do
with your own
ecology of fear?

The Study

There is the silence of an August
afternoon, the lake gun-bright

and still. The silence of the oysterman's
laundry: white socks, a blue shirt
strung across two fence posts.
Empty oyster shells
piled on the beach.

There is the silence of a trap, metal
teeth sprung and bit,

the silence after the rifle has fired,
its black eye pointed
at the ground.

There is the silence draining
from the wolf's eyes, the blood
bubbling from the hole like
a spring.

Between the farmer's house
and the flute player's house
a wolf pisses along
the property line.

There is the silence of a fawn,
whole and wet and speckled
as a fish, slicking the moss
with afterbirth.

The brittle silence of the road sign,
Wolf Creek, pointing to a creek
with no wolves.

The yawning silence of snow
covering the beach without tracks.

After the bounties, the insects
trained the silence, clicking
their laws, the forest thinking,
trying to remember its name.

At the End of the Road, at the Edge of the Sea

Love, remember what we gathered?
A shirt full of chanterelles emptied

in a wooden bowl on the kitchen table.
A bucketful of purple plums, split

and drying on racks. My body wedged
in the crook of two branches, I tossed

you apples below. You carved the bluish-white
flesh of the greenling I caught from the rocky

island where seals gather, heave their fat
in sun and circle, watching our arrival.

That 3am morning we woke for low-tide
clams, stood in that sea of fog

thickening each splash, our bodies
banked towards hush— hiss of barnacles,

bubbles where a clam burped, splash
of a seal somewhere off shore. Burst

of a whale exhaling and fog swallowing
the distance. A drone and rise

of wolf-song from far, shiver
of your hand finding

mine. We drank the sounds and tried to eat
our way to belonging. You stirred paella

with what we gathered—added saffron
you brought from home in Spain.

We ate by firelight, our old dog
licked the plates.

Shadow into Wolf

On the long low-tide of seal spit, I studied just beyond
the horizon
of sight—a dark twist of driftwood, black against the sandy bank
and shag
of cedar. Thought it's just like my mind
to make
a branch a wolf snout, profile with two ears pricked
towards
our boat where you load waterproof bags and I rest
a flash.
I backed away from the killdeer's broken wing dance,
gave
her nesting space, found this water-worn cedar log to sit
a spell.
And like a dream swims up to waking, I saw that branch rise and
all at once
become an actual black wolf watching you load our boat.
Thought
it's just like a wolf to sit beyond the horizon of sight, to shapeshift, to
yank
the mind towards what it fears or yearns for. And just like a wolf to stand up
full
in bodied toothy fact, cut a hole in the forest, all the gathered
shade
and shadow, turn back to trees and leave me
wondering
what I saw and how I might tell it.

ABOUT THE AUTHOR

Anne Haven McDonnell lives in Santa Fe, NM where she teaches as associate professor in English and Creative Writing at the Institute of American Indian Arts. She migrates to the coastal northwest most summers. Her poetry has been published in *Orion Magazine*, *The Georgia Review*, *Nimrod International Journal of Prose and Poetry*, *Alpinist Magazine*, *Terrain.org*, and elsewhere. Her poems won the fifth annual *Terrain.org* poetry prize and second place for the Gingko international ecopoetry prize. Anne has been a writer-in-residence at the Andrews Forest Writers' Residency and the Sitka Center for Art and Ecology.

www.ingramcontent.com/pod-product-compliance
Lightning Source LLC
Chambersburg PA
CBHW022135280326

41933CB00007B/710